THE WISDOM OF THE EARLY BUDDHISTS

THE AUTHOR

Geoffrey Parrinder is Professor of the Comparative Study of Religions in the University of London. After ordination he spent twenty years teaching in West Africa and studying African religions, and became the founder member of the Department of Religious Studies in the University College of Ibadan, Nigeria. He has travelled widely in Africa and in India, Pakistan, Sri Lanka, Burma, Iran, Israel, Jordan and Turkey and held lecturing appointments in Australia, America and India, and at Oxford. He is the author of many books on world religions which have been translated into eight languages.

THE WISDOM OF THE
EARLY BUDDHISTS

COMPILED BY
GEOFFREY PARRINDER

A NEW DIRECTIONS BOOK

Manufactured in the United States of America
First published clothbound and as New Directions Paperbook 444 in 1977 by arrangement with Sheldon Press, London

Library of Congress Cataloging in Publication Data

Main entry under title:

The Wisdom of the early Buddhists.
    (A New Directions Book)
    1. Gautama Buddha—Teachings.   I. Parrinder,
Edward Geoffrey.
BQ915.W57   294.3'4   77-7945
ISBN 0-8112-0666-1
ISBN 0-8112-0667-x pbk.

New Directions Books are published for James Laughlin by New Directions Publishing Corporation, 333 Sixth Avenue, New York 10014

TABLE OF CONTENTS

THE WISDOM OF
THE EARLY BUDDHISTS

*

BUDDHA AND BUDDHISM

THE WISDOM OF
THE EARLY BUDDHISTS

THE BUDDHA was one of the greatest teachers of mankind, revered for over two thousand years by countless millions, and today many people all over the world are interested in his teachings. Like some other religious leaders, the Buddha never wrote a book and the many stories and sayings connected with him were written down by early or later followers. Even more than with the Gospels, these teachings were the product of the early church and reflected the concerns of developing Buddhism.

Many discourses and sermons were attributed to the Buddha but they were lengthy, repetitive and clearly enlarged by disciples. It is not easy to get back to the original message, though occasionally it seems to sparkle sharply. The canonical scriptures of even the more conservative southern Buddhists, the Theravada, followers of the Teaching of the Elders, are several times the length of the Bible and they seem to have been added to freely. Scribes used a common phrase, 'thus have I heard', but they did not hesitate to develop or change a tradition if they thought it could be improved. Moreover there was a lapse of several centuries between the Buddha and writing the scriptures, while the oldest manuscript that exists, a version of the short Dhamma-pada, 'virtue path', in the Gandhari language, is dated from the first or second century A.D.

The scriptures contain many legends about the Buddha, which may seem to be historically unreliable while occasionally preserving grains of fact. But legends reflect the faith of the early community and are invaluable in revealing religious concerns. In this selection we shall find legends of the birth, enlightenment and death of the Buddha, and though a critic may doubt whether the historical Buddha really did speak of descending from heaven and declaring as a newborn babe that he was chief in the world, Buddhists have believed these stories from the earliest centuries and they have shaped the faith that made Buddhism a world religion.

Books on Buddhism for the West often try to ignore the legend, or merely trace social and economic determinants for this religion. Selections of teachings have been made which are either unattached anthologies from the Buddha and later monks, or brief statements of abstract ideas. Yet the major parts of the scriptures, the Dialogues (Sutta), and especially the Long Group (Digha Nikaya), contain many stories as well as much early Buddhist doctrine. As narratives these discourses have been popular down the ages, and if they can be located and abbreviated they may be effective means of presenting the wisdom of the early Buddhists to a wider world.

The one whom we call *the* Buddha is believed to have been one in a series of such teachers and saviours, but since he is the only Buddha of this present world era of nearly half a million years, for all practical purposes he is the Buddha for our time. There are references to Buddhas long ago, and hope of a Buddha to come, Maitreya, and as in other religions there is the notion of golden ages in the past and expectation of better times in the future. But 'in this gracious era the Exalted One has now arisen in the world as a Worthy One and Supreme Buddha'.

The name Buddha is a religious title, the 'Enlightened' or 'Awakened', comparable to the title Christ, 'Anointed'. His personal name was Siddhartha (in Sanskrit; Siddhattha in the Pali scriptural language of the southern school), but this name is rarely used. More frequent is Gotama (in Pali; Gautama in Sanskrit), which was the family name, while in the northern schools he was often given the clan title, Shakya-muni, 'the sage of the Shakyas'.

Several titles are used in the scriptures. One is Bhagava, meaning 'exalted', teacher, Master or Lord. More enigmatic is Tathagata, usually derived from words for 'thus come' or 'thus gone', and apparently meaning 'one who has come and gone like former Buddhas', with the perennial truth, path and goal. To render these titles simply as 'teacher', indicating the original Gotama, would inadequately represent the faith of the early Buddhists who recorded these sayings; hence I have generally rendered them as Master or Buddha, the latter especially after his enlightenment.

It is common nowadays for Buddhist apologists, in East and West, to claim that the Buddha was only a man, or a man like us, but no Buddhist thought this in the previous two thousand years, since the Buddha

5

was for him the object of faith and the means of salvation. Even the thirteenth-century Japanese reformer Nichiren, who rejected many of the later developments and celestial beings of northern Buddhism in favour of a return to the Buddha, saw him on the Vulture Peak surrounded by thousands of gods and men as depicted in the Lotus scripture.

Buddhism has often been called agnostic or even atheistic, in modern times, and it did reject or ignore much Hindu theology. Hindu gods appear in the Theravada scriptures, Brahma, Indra and the like, but they are lay figures or attendants upon the Buddha who occupies the centre of the stage. None of these gods is the Supreme Being, and the Buddha did not acknowledge them as such. He himself was not called a god, indeed that would be unworthy, since the gods are not yet fully enlightened but are caught up in the round of transmigration. But the Buddha is above all these beings and is called 'Teacher of gods and men'. Functionally he is the Supreme Being, and in a confession of faith that dates from early years men cried, 'I go to the Buddha for refuge', as Hindus go to Krishna or Shiva for refuge.

With the Buddha there is the Doctrine or Truth (*dharma* or *dhamma*) and the Order (*Sangha*). Dharma is a Protean term: doctrine, teaching, law, norm, virtue, righteousness, religion, truth. Nineteenth-century Western interpreters tended to make the Doctrine into simple moral precepts, the Buddha being a mere man, and this suited utilitarian agnostics who would have been shocked to see inside a Buddhist

6

pagoda, with its idols and joss-sticks. Buddhism seemed to them a system of self-improvement, without the superstitions of God and the soul, but some modern experts state matters differently. 'Bitter and incredible as it must seem to the contemporary mind', writes Professor Edward Conze, 'Buddhism bases itself first of all on the revelation of the Truth by an omniscient being, known as "the Buddha", and secondly on the spiritual intuition of saintly beings'.[1] Buddhism is not self-salvation, which can be produced by any Tom, Dick or Harry, but acceptance of the Truth revealed by the Buddha and given by religious experts in the scriptures.

The Order may at first have indicated the whole community of believers, but it came to denote particularly the inner circle of dedicated monks. The word 'monk' may suggest to Western minds a body of men shut off from the world in an enclosed or fortress monastery. I prefer to call them 'brothers', like the followers of Francis of Assisi, little poor men, holy 'beggars' (*bhikkhus*). They wandered freely through the world, yet sought detachment from its lusts and follies, having gone out from home to the homeless life in a search for truth and peace. Their houses were places of retreat, like the *ashrams* of Hindu forest sages, and they have traditionally been open to the laity for spiritual discipline in the rainy seasons. The Sangha has been the inner church of Buddhism, though today in lands where it has been attacked or abolished the fate of Buddhism depends on the lay followers.

1. *Buddhist Thought in India.* University of Michigan 1967, p. 30.

The date of the Buddha is uncertain, though it was in pre-Christian times. Sinhalese Buddhists have a tradition that his death occurred in 544 B.C., but others think it was just a hundred years before the great Buddhist emperor Ashoka, who ruled over most of India from about 270 B.C. Many scholars accept the Buddha's dates as 563–483 B.C., though these are rather too precise and probably the fifth or fourth centuries are near enough.

He was born in northern India or the foothills of Nepal, to a princely family. This meant that he belonged to the Kshatriya warrior-ruler caste or class, and not to the Brahmin priestly class. The Brahmins were responsible for recitation of the sacred texts, the Vedas, and for offering sacrifices, but the Buddhists say little of either. Even the discussions of groups of Brahmin philosophers, which had been going on for centuries and are preserved in the Upanishads, receive little attention in the Buddhist dialogues. The Buddha, unlike the Upanishadic philosophers, does not seem to have been concerned with the Absolute or Brahman, or the cosmic self (*atman*), though he did refuse to locate an individual and eternal self. But the ruling class seem to have retained some ancient Indian beliefs, notably in reincarnation or transmigration, which they may have absorbed through intermarriage with members of earlier Indian races, and these are taken for granted by Buddhists. The Upanishads themselves admit that knowledge of reincarnation was unknown formerly to the Brahmins but guarded by the rulers.[2]

2. See *The Wisdom of the Forest*. New Directions 1976, pp. 11, 16, 58.

A contemporary and perhaps earlier religious movement among the rulers was that of the Jains, called after their teachers, the Jinas, 'conquerors'. The Jains are claimed to be a long succession, like the Buddhas who are also called 'conquerors'. Their religion is eternal, since not only are there twenty-four Jinas going back many millions of years in present eons, but countless others in former ages. Their latest Jina was surnamed Maha-vira, 'mighty hero', sometimes dated 599–527 or 540–468 B.C., and parallel to the Buddha in some events of his life. The Jains have also taught reincarnation and final Nirvana, but they practised severe asceticism, whereas Buddhism claims to be the Middle Way, between extremes of asceticism and sensuality.

Siddhartha's father was the raja Suddhodana, and his mother Maya, living in the town of Kapilavastu. Although legend increasingly added miraculous elements to the infancy stories, the child was born in wedlock and it was not a virginal conception. The birth is said to have taken place in the Lumbini park and at these sacred sites, together with the places of the Enlightenment and death, the emperor Ashoka caused monuments to be built. Tradition says that Siddhartha, like Mahavira, was married and had a child, and then at the age of twenty-nine he renounced wife and baby to take up the homeless life in search of peace. Central to tradition are the Four Signs, of age, sickness, death and a monk, which so impressed Gotama with the suffering and transience of life that he abandoned everything to find out their cause.

9

He gave up his possessions and rich clothing, and wandered from teacher to teacher, sitting at the feet of Brahmins and yogis to hear their views, but found no satisfaction. A popular story, depicted in painting and sculpture also, shows Gotama practising extreme asceticism and becoming like a skeleton, but then abandoning such austerity for the Middle Way. Eventually he was 'enlightened', became Buddha, under a sacred pipal tree, said to be the Bo-tree at Gaya, in modern Bihar. Here he gained perfect knowledge of all the past, present and future, and was omniscient in more than divine fashion. This was virtual Nirvana, extinction of all craving, and there would be a temptation to remain in this bliss. But tradition says that the gods were so alarmed at the prospect that they sent their chief, Brahma, to implore the Buddha to preach his wisdom for the welfare of mankind, and thus he became an evangelist. There probably was a struggle between the joy and calm of attainment and recognition of the needs of others and desire to tell the message. Buddhist traditions speak of certain 'separate' Pratyeka Buddhas, who lived like lonely rhinoceroses, but their Buddha was interested in human welfare and spent many years in teaching.

From Gaya the Buddha went to the sacred city of Benares or Varanasi and a little way to the north, in a deer park at Sarnath, he preached his first sermon, called Setting in Motion the Wheel of Truth. The site is still marked by the lofty remains of a monument erected by Ashoka. Here the Buddha set out the basic Four Noble Truths: the universal fact of suffering, its cause in craving, its cessation by the stopping of craving, and the way to achieve this by the Noble Eightfold Path. This Path is in eight terms of Right: right views, motive, speech, action, livelihood, effort, mindfulness and contemplation. These statements are basic to all forms of Buddhism and may be claimed as original to the Buddha himself, though later teachers elaborated them. They are part of the Dharma, the doctrine and truth, and the fundamental law of the universe.

The Buddha gathered round him both monks and laymen and in early days he moved from place to place. Hence we often read of him staying in some mango grove or royal park. Later life became more sedentary and both solitaries and communities would need 'a village nearby for support', but the villagers were glad to have the holiness and learning of the Order at hand to bring them credit and blessing and education for their children. The Buddha wandered round north India and towns are mentioned which were famous already or became so by connection with his history: Benares, Rajagaha, Nalanda, Vesali, Kusinara.

Finally he passed away, and amid the legend there are interesting pointers to history. It is said that he had been ill, probably with one of the forms of dysentery which are endemic in the tropics and of which the Prophet Muhammad also died. The immediate cause of death, at about eighty years of age, is said to have been eating tainted pork provided by a smith named Chunda. The Buddha was vowed to abstain from taking life, but he was not a strict vegetarian and was bound to take whatever was given. Some English scholars have translated pork as 'truffles', perhaps thinking the former to be unworthy of the Buddha but, as a French scholar has remarked, truffles may be more elegant but are not more digestible.

The Buddha died at Kusinara, which the text apologetically calls 'a wattle-and-daub town in the midst of the jungle', no doubt thinking that the death ought to have occurred at a great and holy city like Benares. But the memory of this humble location supports the truth of the story. The Buddha's remains after cremation are said to have been divided between eight towns, and the fact that there were relics to be divided shows that the Buddha was regarded as a real personage. He had already attained Nirvana at his Enlightenment but had deferred final separation from the world and now entered Pari-nirvana, 'complete Nirvana'. The Buddha's final words, typical of his attitude to the transience of life, are said to have been: 'All composite things are decaying. Work out your salvation with diligence.' The second sentence is missing in some versions, which are content with the simple statement of the facts of life. But the words about striving, 'work out your salvation', have endeared Buddhism to Western moralists who like to think of it as a non-theistic system of self-improvement, though all forms of Buddhism are far more than this.

In this selection traditional accounts of the Buddha's birth and enlightenment are put first, and his death last, to provide a framework for the stories and discourses. Some of these are put in his own mouth and others come from disciples, but both refer to other Buddhas and celestial beings. One eminent British scholar in the early years of this century called the notion of these Buddhas a spreading weed which covered up much of the earlier teaching, while other writers have seen in them the salvation of Buddhism in developing into a religion. But, as we have seen, the notion of successive teachers and saviours, Jinas and Buddhas, is very old in India, and the story of the Buddha cannot be disentangled from the faith of early Buddhists. Here enough has been given to place the Buddha in a great succession, which is not unreasonable.

The stories are told in prose and verse and it is difficult to know which is older. An eminent translator, Mrs Rhys Davids, introducing the Kindred Sayings (Samyutta Nikaya) remarked, 'Mythical and folk-lore drapery are wrapped about many of the sayings here ascribed to the Buddha. And in nearly all of them, if any represent genuine prose utterances, they have become deflected in the prism of memorializing verse, and to that extent artificial. Nevertheless, the matter of them is of the stamp of the oldest doctrine known to us, and from them a fairly complete synopsis of the ancient Dhamma might be compiled.'[3] Probably the Buddha did not speak in verse, but some of the short verses that have been preserved may represent early efforts at remembering his teachings

3. Preface to *The Book of Kindred Sayings*. Pali Text Society 1917, p. vii.

in easy forms. There is also a great deal of prose, which is very prosy, and not necessarily any nearer to what the Buddha actually said, but one has to select what appear to be major interests of Buddhism.

The narratives of the Buddha's travels and discourses given in this selection are taken chiefly from the Long Group, which is the first in the central collection of Buddhist dialogues according to Theravada Buddhism. They associate the Buddha with different places and people, and reveal in questions and answers what were the concerns of early southern Buddhism. The life of the monk is justified and shown to be peaceful. The aversion of the Buddha to idle speculation is represented as characteristic of him: whether the soul is eternal or not, or partly eternal or not, or formed or formless. It is sometimes claimed that the Buddha denied the existence of the soul or self, but what was criticized was both speculation and identifications of the soul with any of the mortal human elements. As Dr Conze says: 'The Buddha never taught that the self "is not", but only that "it cannot be apprehended".'[4]

The Buddha is depicted as talking with many classes of people, from kings to courtesans, and from priests to blacksmiths. The Brahmins, priests or scholars, who claimed to be the highest class in Indian society, were especially important. They would most easily challenge Buddhist teaching where it conflicted with Hindu ideas, and claims to superiority laid them open to criticism. The Buddha came from the warrior-ruler class and there was traditional rivalry with the Brah-

4. *Buddhist Thought in India*, p. 39.

14

mins, like that between church and state, or pope and emperor. In a dialogue with the priest Sona-danda he is led to admit that colour, birth and priestly training are secondary, and that what really count are virtue and wisdom. But other priests objected to this and to Buddhist attack on animal sacrifice.

Similarly Buddhist leaders discounted miracles, extreme austerities and speculations, with which both common people and scholars were preoccupied. They taught the Middle Way, the Eightfold Path, and unconcern with unprofitable questions. The constant refrain at the end of discussion is that the truth has now been revealed, the right path indicated and the lamp lit in the dark, by the unsurpassed guide to mortals, the teacher of gods and men. The questioners take the Buddha, the Teaching and the Order for refuge, and enrol themselves as disciples for life.

Some of the disciples, like Ananda, Sariputta, Moggallana and Kumara, have discourses attributed to them and some taught after the Buddha's death. But while most of the dialogues are formally referred to the Buddha himself, they come to us as the teaching of Theravada Buddhism. Some of the instructions were especially given to laymen, like the householder Sigala, and show the increasing effect of Buddhist teaching upon the community and the need to provide rules for ordinary followers as well as members of the Order.

Buddhists accepted general Indian beliefs in transmigration or rebirth, with notions both of rounds of existence for the individual and cycles of emergence and dissolution for the world. There are collections of popular tales, the Jatakas or Birth Stories, which tell of the past births of the Buddha-to-be some five hundred and fifty times in human, animal or angelic forms. The Jatakas are part of the canon of scripture, but they are a medley of faith and folklore, and secondary to the discourses in matters of doctrine and morals. They are not referred to in this selection because of their length and content.

Buddhism has taught a way of deliverance or salvation from the round of existences into Nirvana. This word was used by Jains and Buddhists before it entered into Hindu thought through the Bhagavad Gita. It is sometimes translated as 'extinction' or 'annihilation', but it is important to note what is annihilated. Nirvana is derived from a root *va*, meaning 'to blow', and *nir* or *nis* is the negative; so Nir-vana means 'blown out'. The comparison is to a lamp blown out, and indicates the passions with the individuality which is attached to them. These are extinguished in Nirvana, the unconditioned and indescribable peace and bliss which is attained at enlightenment. It is not annihilation of the eternal essence or reality, nor is it, as some dictionaries put it, 'absorption into the supreme spirit'. Rather it is the goal of life, the ultimate bliss, attained by most people after many lives.

Nirvana is not given much description, nor could it be, but in the later Questions of King Milinda there are attempts to indicate its state:

As a lotus flower is unstained by water, so Nirvana

is unstained by defilements; as cool water removes heat and thirst, so Nirvana removes the fever of passion and the craving for becoming; as medicine cures sickness and gives health, so Nirvana puts an end to all suffering; as space is not born or dies, is not conquered or stolen, neither is Nirvana; as a mountain peak is lofty and inaccessible, so Nirvana is exalted and inaccessible to the passions.

These and other early Buddhist teachings are characteristic of Theravada Buddhism. With kindred schools this came to be called Hina-yana, the 'lesser vehicle' of salvation, by rivals who claimed to have a more universal appeal. The Theravada reject this claim, along with the title Hinayana. They are the Buddhists today of Sri Lanka, Burma, Thailand, Cambodia and Laos, and recently have converted several million Indians.

The Maha-yana, 'great vehicle', set out their claim to universality in a distinctive scripture, The Lotus of the Wonderful Law, composed perhaps about the second century A.D. This work declares that the Buddhas do not bring salvation by a lesser vehicle, and it gives an account of a schism with the withdrawal of five thousand proud monks, nuns and laymen, whom the Buddha is said to have described to Sariputta as chaff and trash. The Mahayana developed ideas of other Buddhas and Buddhas-to-be, Buddha-fields, the Pure Land and the Western Paradise. Countless supernatural beings fill the later scriptures and temples, and Buddhism absorbed much of the popular religion of China, Japan, Korea and Tibet.

Perhaps partly against lush Buddhology, Mahayana philosophy developed a doctrine of the Void, meaning that ultimate reality has no characteristics or substance. Nothing could be stated baldly, not only transmigration and Nirvana, but even salvation and the Buddha himself. Then in Zen Buddhism there is a rejection of words and letters, even of scripture, and search for the Buddha-nature within, as illustrated in *The Wisdom of the Zen Masters* in this series. Mahayana philosophy seems more akin to Hindu and parts of Chinese thought, while Theravada appears less speculative though still religious.

It is said that there were eighteen Hinayana sects but Theravada is their sole survivor today. It claims to be nearer to the teaching of the Buddha and his immediate followers than Mahayana, but it is a religion with many visible expressions of faith in pagodas and dagobas, paintings and images. When he went to Burma, says the anthropologist Melford Spiro, he expected to find a religion different from others, without belief in supernatural beings, the soul, happiness or a future life. When he arrived there he found he had been wrongly informed, for Buddhists differ little from people in general, and their beliefs confirm deep-seated human needs for faith in powers and truths that make for moral and holy living.[5]

The limited number of texts used here are but a small part of the extensive Theravada scriptures, which are full of repetition. This was useful for teaching and learning by heart but it is tedious in books, and even

5. *Buddhism and Society*. Allen and Unwin 1971, p. 10.

standard complete editions resort to asterisks to avoid reprinting the same statements with slight variations. These teachings of the early Buddhists are of great importance, and have been venerated for thousands of years, but it is a fallacy that religious books necessarily make interesting reading, for many of them are obscure and tedious. The Upanishads wryly remark that 'the gods love the cryptic and dislike the obvious'. The early Buddhists were not often cryptic but they were very wordy, and this has put their works beyond the reach of most readers even in translation.

For nearly a hundred years the Pali Text Society has been publishing at intervals English translations of the canon of Theravada and this is now almost complete. The earlier volumes in particular are in graceful English and have been used extensively here. It is to open these beautiful and absorbing dialogues to the Western public, in abbreviated and direct form, that this version of the Wisdom of the Early Buddhists has been made. Graceful language, humane spirit, religious devotion and moral endeavour appear as characteristic products of Theravada Buddhism.

BUDDHA AND BUDDHISM

THE BUDDHA was staying at a cottage in a wood and many brothers who had returned from an alms-tour sat in a pavilion nearby discussing births in other lives. The Master with supernatural hearing knew of their conversation and went to ask if they would like instruction, and at their request he said: It is many ages since the first Buddha Vipassi arose in the world and he was followed by five others. In this gracious era I have arisen in the world as a Worthy One and Supreme Buddha, in a noble clan and to a family surnamed Gotama. My father is the raja Suddhodana, my mother is his wife Maya, and their seat is the town of Kapilavastu. My chief attendant is Ananda and principal disciples Sariputta and Moggallana. My leaving the world, becoming a recluse, travail, enlightenment under the Bo-tree and setting in motion the Wheel of Truth will be told you.

THE MASTER asked Ananda to recount his history and qualities and Ananda said: I heard this face to face from the Lord. He arose mindful and conscious in heaven and descended into his mother's womb, whereupon great splendour appeared in the world surpassing the majesty of the gods and the universe quaked. When the Buddha-to-be entered his mother the gods protected her, she abstained from falsehood

21

and taking life, she had no thought of men, she was in possession of all her senses, was happy and had no sickness, and saw the babe within her body in perfection. Ten months after conception his mother gave birth standing and died seven days later. When the Buddha-to-be was born he was clean and unstained. He stood on his feet, took seven steps, surveyed all quarters and said in a loud voice: I am the chief, eldest and foremost in the world. This is my last birth. There is no more coming to be.

★ III ★

THE BUDDHA told the brothers of the Four Signs which appeared to Vipassi and all Buddhas: As he was driving through the park he saw an old man leaning on a staff and asked his charioteer what he had done to be like that. He replied: He is an aged man. Vipassi asked: Shall I also become aged? And being told that it was so he returned to the palace brooding and depressed. Another day he saw a sick man, and asked if sickness could come to him, and returned brooding and depressed. Then he saw a corpse on a funeral pyre and asked: Am I too subject to death? Being told that all men are mortal, he went back brooding and depressed. Finally he saw a monk, with shaven head and yellow robe, and was told that he was a wanderer who had gone forth to a religious life, to good actions, harmless behaviour and kindness to all creatures. He said: That is excellent. Take the carriage back, but I will cut off my hair now, don the yellow robe and go out to the homeless state.

ONE DAY the Buddha dressed early in the morning to go out for almsfood. In the evening he went with Ananda to bathe and stood in a single robe drying his limbs. A number of the brothers were talking in the hermitage and the Master stood outside, coughed and knocked on the door. He asked the subject of their conversation and they answered: Our talk that was interrupted was about the Lord himself. So he told them of his Noble Quest in these words: Before my Enlightenment, while I was still the Buddha-to-be, being myself subject to birth, I sought out the nature of birth, being subject to old age I sought out the nature of old age, of sickness, death, sorrow and impurity. Then I thought: What if I, having seen the wretchedness of birth, were to seek the unborn, the supreme peace of Nirvana?

THERE WAS a Jain apologist to whom the Master spoke of his detachment from pleasure and pain and his Renunciation: Before my Enlightenment, while I was still the Buddha-to-be and not fully awakened, I thought that life was oppressive in a house full of dust. Living in a house it is not easy to lead a full, pure and polished religious life, but the open air is better. Suppose I cut off my hair and beard, put on yellow robes and go from the house to a homeless life? So after a time, while I was a young black-haired lad, though my unwilling parents wept, I shaved my head and beard, put on yellow robes and left home for the homeless life.

⋆ VI ⋆

To the brothers the Master recounted his visits to various teachers: When I went forth to seek for the good and perfect path to peace I approached a recluse named Alara. I said: Reverend Sir, I wish to practise the religious life and discipline. Alara replied that his teaching could be understood quickly by an intelligent man, and I mastered it very soon, as far as lip service went. I approached him again and asked: What is the extent of your doctrine? Then Alara proclaimed the attainment of the state of Nothingness, but this too I realized and attained. Alara set me, his pupil, on the same level as himself, but I considered that his teaching did not lead to absence of passion, tranquillity, higher knowledge or Nirvana, but only to nothingness. So not getting enough from this doctrine I disregarded and turned away from it.

⋆ VII ⋆

The Master, seeking for the good and perfect path to peace, approached a teacher named Uddaka and asked to practise his religious life and discipline. He quickly mastered it and realized a state of Neither-consciousness-nor-unconsciousness. Uddaka said: As I am, so are you. Come, let the two of us together look after my disciples. But the Master thought: This teaching does not lead to absence of passion, tranquillity, higher knowledge or Nirvana. So not getting enough from this doctrine I shall disregard and turn away from it.

★ VIII ★

THE MASTER SAID: As I was seeking for the perfect path to peace, I walked through the country and arrived near a camp at Uruvela. There was a delightful woodland grove, with a clear flowing river, a good ford and a village nearby for support. This struck me as a good place for a young man intent on the quest and I sat down.

On another occasion the Master spoke of his meditation: I set my teeth, pressed my tongue to my palate, restrained and controlled my mind, so that sweat flowed freely. My body was unquiet but these painful feelings did not overpower my mind. Then I restrained breathing in and out of the mouth and nose, until there was a loud noise in my ears like the roar of a blacksmith's bellows. I held my breath till people said I was dying or dead. But my body was unquiet and these painful feelings did not overpower my mind.

★ IX ★

THE MASTER SAID: Five monks sat near me, thinking that when I attained the Truth I would tell it to them. I decided to take only small amounts of food, as many beans as my hollowed palm would hold. My body became thin, my ribs stuck out like the beams of an old shed, my eyes sank low like a deep well, my skull became like a cracked gourd, and when I tried to

25

touch the skin of my stomach I caught hold of my spine. Then I thought: Ascetics in the past suffered severe pains without attaining enlightenment, perhaps there is another way to it which cannot be followed while my body is weak. I got up and took rice-milk from the daughter of the village overseer and ate some beans. Then the five monks left me in disgust, saying that I had given up striving and returned to a life of abundance.

⋆ X ⋆

THE MASTER described his Enlightenment: When I had taken food and gained strength, without sensual desires or evil thoughts, I entered the first state of meditation arising from seclusion and reasoning which is joyous and blissful. Next I entered the second state, born of concentration and beyond reasoning. Then I entered the third state, attentive and conscious, with equal mind to joy or aversion. Finally I entered the fourth state, beyond pain and pleasure, entirely pure and mindful.

I remembered all my former existences, in the first watch of the night. I saw all beings arising and passing away according to their deeds, in the middle watch. Being liable to birth because of self, to age and sorrow and death, I sought the unborn and undecaying and undying. I attained this in the last watch of the night and won the stainless, the freedom from bondage, Nirvana. Knowledge and vision came to me. This is unshakeable freedom. This is my last birth. There is no more coming to be.

THE BUDDHA, now fully enlightened, told of a problem: It occurred to me that this Truth I have won is deep, difficult to perceive and understand, while the world delights in sensual pleasure. If I were to teach the Truth and others did not understand, that would be weariness and vexation. Then it occurred to the chief of the gods, Brahma, that the world would be lost and destroyed if the perfect one, the Buddha, was not inclined to teach the Truth. So Brahma vanished from heaven and appeared before me, with robe over one shoulder and hands joined and said: Let the Lord teach the Truth, for there are beings with but little dust in their eyes who will grow if they hear it. Then I surveyed the world with the compassionate eye of a Buddha, and as in a pond a few blue, red or white lotuses rise out of the water undefiled, so I saw beings with little dust and good disposition, and I addressed Brahma with this verse:

> The Doors of No More Death
> are open for those who hear,
> let them put forth their faith.

* XII *

THE BUDDHA SAID: I considered who would understand the Truth quickly and I thought of Alara, but I was told he had passed away seven days before. Then I thought that Uddaka would understand quickly, but was told that he had passed away last night. Then I thought of the five monks and hearing that they were at Benares I set out towards it. On the way I met a naked ascetic, Upaka, who said: Sir, your face is very bright and clear, who is your teacher or what Doctrine do you profess? I replied in these verses:

I am the Victor over all,
omniscient and pure in all,
freed from craving, leaving all,
know by myself and point to none.

To turn the Wheel of Truth
Benares I shall find,
to beat the Drum of No More Death
before a world that's blind.

★ XIII ★

WHEN THE BUDDHA arrived at Benares the five monks were in a deer park at Sarnath. Seeing him coming they agreed not to greet or serve him, since he had gone back to a life of abundance. But as he drew near they were not able to keep their agreement, some made a seat ready, some brought water to wash his feet, others took his bowl and robe, and all called him: Your Reverence. The Buddha replied: Do not call me Your Reverence. The Buddha is perfect, fully self-awakened. I have found the deathless and I teach the Truth. If you follow this you will soon realize here and now the goal of religion for which young men of good family leave home for the homeless life, and you will abide in it.

To THE FIVE MONKS the Buddha preached his first sermon, Setting in Motion the Wheel of Truth: Avoiding the extremes of sensuality and self-torture, the Buddha has gained the knowledge of the Middle Way, which brings insight, calm and Nirvana. What is the Middle Way? It is the Noble Eightfold Path.

Consider the Four Noble Truths. This is the Noble Truth of Pain: birth, age, sickness, death, sorrow and despair are painful. This is the Noble Truth of the Cause of Pain: it is craving, which leads to rebirth, pleasure and passion, existence and non-existence. This is the Noble Truth of the Cessation of Pain: it is the cessation of craving without remainder, forsaking, detachment and release from it. This is the Noble Truth of the Way that leads to the Cessation of Pain: it is the Noble Eightfold Path.

* XV *

WHAT IS the Noble Eightfold Path? It is: Right Views, Right Motive, Right Speech, Right Action, Right Livelihood, Right Effort, Right Mindfulness, Right Contemplation. Right Views give the knowledge of Pain, its Cause, Cessation, and the Path. Right Motive gives aspiration to renunciation and benevolence. Right Speech abstains from lies and slander. Right Action abstains from stealing, killing and indulgence. Right Livelihood follows right pursuits. Right Effort turns against evil states and towards good. Right Mindfulness looks on body and mind with self-possession. Right Contemplation rises above evil and abides in equanimity and bliss.

THE BUDDHA preached to the five monks in a second sermon on the Marks of Non-Soul. The body is not the soul, for if it were the body would not be subject to sickness, but it is not possible to say of the body, let it be thus or not thus. The feelings are not the soul, perception is not the soul, the elements are not the soul, consciousness is not the soul, for the same reasons.

What do you think, monks? Is the body permanent or impermanent? They replied: It is impermanent. He asked: Is the impermanent painful or pleasant? They answered: It is painful. The Buddha retorted: But is it fitting to consider what is impermanent and painful as myself and the soul? They answered, No.

The Buddha asked the same questions of the feelings, perception, the elements and the consciousness. In none of them was the soul found. Then the five monks rejoiced at this teaching and their hearts were freed from faults.

FOR SOME FORTY YEARS the Buddha and his followers travelled round northern India, staying at various places and teaching. One day he was going along the high road between Rajagaha and Nalanda with about five hundred brothers, and behind them came a religious beggar, Suppiya, and his young disciple Brahma-datta, 'god-given'. Suppiya was criticizing the Buddha, the Teaching and the Order of brothers in many ways, but Brahma-datta praised all three. At night they all stayed at a royal rest-house and continued discussion. In the morning the Buddha found the brothers talking about these criticisms and he said: If outsiders speak against me, the Teaching or the Order, you should not be angry for that would prevent your own self-conquest. Similarly if they praise us. But you should find out what is false or true, and acknowledge the fact. And even in praise it is only of trifling matters that an unconverted man might speak of me.

* XVIII *

THE BUDDHA described his outward life and behaviour and those of his followers, saying: An unconverted man might say that the recluse Gotama has renounced killing living things, putting aside the cudgel and sword, and ashamed of roughness he is kind and compassionate to all living creatures. Or an unconverted man might say that Gotama has put away stealing, unchastity, lies, slander, quarrelling, rudeness in speech, frivolous talk, gluttony, pleasures, bribes, cheating, robbery, murder, violence, and so on. Such and many more are the things that an unconverted man might say in praise of the Buddha.

* XIX *

THE BUDDHA continued: There are other things, beyond the trifling details of mere morality, which are hard to understand. There are scholars who speculate about the origins of things, holding that the soul and the world are eternal, or partly eternal and partly not, but how do they arrive at this conclusion? There comes a time when the world passes away but purified beings remain in the World of Light. Another time comes when the world begins to evolve again and the palace of the gods appears but it is empty. Then some being whose time in the World of Light is exhausted comes to life in the palace of the gods and says: I am Brahma, the Great God, All-seeing, Creator and Ruler of all. When other beings appear they accept this claim, and consider that Brahma will remain for ever but that they are created and of limited life, and so do those who hold that the soul and the world are partly eternal and partly not.

★ XX ★

THE BUDDHA continued: Scholars speak in sixteen ways of the state of the soul after death. They say that it has form or is formless; has and has not form, or neither has nor has not form; it is finite or infinite; or both or neither; it has one mode of consciousness or several; has limited consciousness or infinite; is happy or miserable; or both or neither.

The Buddha knows that these are speculations and what the result will be. He knows other things far beyond, and is not puffed up because he has realized a way of escape from them. He understands the rise and passing of sensations, their sweetness and danger, and by not grasping them he is set free. These things are profound and difficult, not to be grasped by mere logic. The Buddha has realized this and set it forth, and those who would rightly praise him should speak of this.

32

★XXI★

AJATA-SATTU, king of Magadha, sat on the terrace
roof of his palace with his ministers on the night of the
full moon. The king sang in joy: How lovely is this
moonlit night, where is the sage whom we might call
on to satisfy our hearts? Six ministers spoke of famous
teachers but the king was silent. Then he turned to
Jivaka, the children's doctor, and asked: Why do you
say nothing? Jivaka replied: Sir, the Blessed One, the
Enlightened, is staying in my mango grove with
twelve hundred brothers, and it is said that he is full
of wisdom and goodness, unsurpassed as a guide to
mortals, the teacher of gods and men, a blessed
Buddha. If you visit him your heart will find peace.

★XXII★

KING AJATA-SATTU had five hundred elephants made
ready, with five hundred of his women riding them
while he rode on the state elephant, and with attendants
bearing torches they set out for the mango grove.
When the king drew near he was seized with fear and
his hair stood on end. Anxious and excited he asked
Jivaka: Are you deceiving me or betraying me to my
enemies? How is it that there is no sound, not even a
sneeze or a cough, in such a large assembly? Jivaka
answered: I would not trick you. Go on, the lamps
are burning in the pavilion. The king went on as far as
his elephant could pass and then proceeded on foot.
The Buddha was sitting against the middle pillar,
facing east, with the brothers around him in perfect
silence, calm as a clear lake. The king stood respect-

33

fully to one side and exclaimed: Would that my son might enjoy such calm as this assembly has!

★ XXIII ★

KING AJATA-SATTU bowed to the Buddha, saluted the brothers with joined hands, and said: I wish to question the Blessed One if he will allow me. He replied: Ask what you wish. The king said: There are many ordinary occupations which bring visible rewards and support of families, but what visible fruit is there of the life of a monk? The Buddha answered: Suppose you have a servant who strives in everything to do your will. And suppose he thinks it strange for you to be a king and powerful, it must be the result of merit, but you are a man and so is he. And suppose he shaves off his hair and beard, dons a yellow robe and is admitted to an Order. And suppose your people tell you this, and say your former servant dwells in solitude and is content with mere food and shelter. Would you tell the man to come back and be a slave again? The king replied: No, we would greet him reverently, give him a lodging and medicine for the sick, and guard him according to custom. The Buddha answered: If that is so, there is some visible reward of the life of a recluse.

★ XXIV ★

KING AJATA-SATTU asked: Can you show me any other fruit of the life of a monk? The Buddha replied: Suppose there appears in the world one who has gained the truth, fully enlightened, a teacher of gods and men, a Buddha. By himself he thoroughly knows

34

face to face the universe, gods and men, princes and people, and having known it he tells others. He proclaims the truth, lovely in its origin, progress and end, in spirit and letter. He makes known the higher life in fullness and purity.

If a householder or one of his children, or a man of lower birth in any class, hears that truth and has faith in the Buddha, then he renounces the hindrances of the world and donning yellow robes goes out to the homeless life. He lives in self-restraint, surrounding himself with good deeds and words, and is altogether happy. He puts away taking life, lays aside the cudgel and sword, and is kind to all living creatures. This is an immediate fruit of the life of a recluse, higher and sweeter than others.

* XXV *

THE BUDDHA said: O king, if a man stood by a clear mountain pool and saw oysters and shells, gravel, pebbles and fishes within it, he would know that the pool was transparent and serene. That would be like the fruit of the life of a recluse.

King Ajata-sattu cried: This is most excellent. It is as if a man were to put up what had been thrown down, reveal what was hidden, point out the road to one that was lost, or bring a lamp into darkness. So the truth has been made known to me by the Blessed One, in many a figure. And now I go to the Blessed One as my refuge, to the Teaching and the Order. May he accept me as a disciple, who from this day forth takes refuge in them as long as life endures. I acknowledge

35

my sins, and may the Blessed One accept me so that in future I may restrain myself from wrong. Now, Lord, we must go, for we are busy and there is much to do. Then king Ajata-sattu, pleased and delighted with the Master's words, rose from his seat, bowed and went away.

★ XXVI ★

THERE WAS a scholar named Pokkhara-sadi who lived on a royal domain and had as pupil a young priest Ambattha. This youth had mastered the scriptures by heart, ritual, chants, exegesis, legends, grammar and sophistry. Pokkhara-sadi heard that the recluse Gotama was staying in the woods with a great company and he said to Ambattha: My dear fellow, go to Gotama and find out whether the great reputation he has is true. Ambattha arose, bowed to his master, entered a chariot drawn by mares, and went to the woods with a retinue of young scholars. There he saw some of the brothers walking up and down and asked: Where is the venerable Gotama, we have come to call on him? They replied: There is his lodging where the door is shut. Go up quietly, cough and knock. Ambattha did so and the Blessed One opened the door for him to enter.

★ XXVII ★

THE YOUNG scholars greeted the Buddha with compliments and sat down, but Ambattha said something civil in an offhand way, fidgeting and walking about while the Master was sitting. The Buddha asked: Is that the way you talk with older teachers, moving about while they sit? Ambattha replied: Certainly not,

36

one speaks to a scholar walking only if he is walking, or sitting when he sits. But with shaven monks, sham friars and menial black fellows, I would talk as I do now. The Master said: But you must have wanted something when you came, you are an ill-bred priest or ill-trained. Ambattha was angry and sneered: Your ruler class is rough and rude, touchy and violent, they are menials and do not respect priests, that is unseemly. The Master replied with this verse:

> The ruler is best among those men
> who trust in birth for nobleness,
> but he is best of gods and men
> who is perfect in wisdom and righteousness.

⋆XXVIII⋆

THE YOUNG PRIEST Ambattha asked: Where are the wisdom and righteousness spoken of in that verse? The Buddha replied: In perfect wisdom and righteousness there is no concern for birth or lineage or the pride which says that you are as worthy as I am or not as worthy. People who talk about marrying and giving in marriage refer to such things, but whoever is bound by notions of birth or social position or marriage connections, is far from the best wisdom and righteousness. It is only by getting rid of such bondage that one can realize for himself the supreme perfection in wisdom and conduct.

⋆XXIX⋆

THE BUDDHA instructed Ambattha in morality, conduct and wisdom. Then he said: Such a man is perfect in wisdom and conduct, but there are four failures from it. If a recluse plunges into the depths of the forest to live on fruit, without having attained perfect wisdom and conduct, he will only be worthy to be a servant of one who has attained them. And if recluses live only on roots, or worship the fire, or build resthouses, without perfect wisdom and conduct, they will only be worthy to be servants. Have you been trained to do any of these things, Ambattha? None of them, he replied. Then the Master said: You have fallen short of proper training and your teacher has wronged you.

* XXX *

AMBATTHA made his farewell, mounted his chariot drawn by mares and went home. His teacher Pokkhara-sadi asked him: Well, did you see Gotama and is he as reputation says? Ambattha replied: Yes, sir, he has all the marks of a great man. Pokkhara-sadi asked: Did you talk to him, and how did the conversation go? Ambattha told him, and Pokkhara-sadi cried: Oh, you wiseacre, you dullard, you expert in the scriptures! A man who does his business like that will be reborn in a state of misery. The sage was angry and kicked Ambattha, and decided to go and call on the Buddha himself.

* XXXI *

POKKHARA-SADI had food made ready and taken on wagons through the night while he followed in his chariot. When he had greeted the Buddha he asked:

Has our pupil, the young priest Ambattha, been here? And did you have any discussion? The Master told him what had been said and the scholar remarked: He is young and foolish, Gotama, please forgive him. The Buddha replied that he was forgiven, and then he discoursed on generosity and right conduct, on the vanity of lust and the advantage of renunciation, and on heaven. Pokkhara-sadi observed that he had all the marks of a great man.

XXXII

WHEN THE BUDDHA perceived that Pokkhara-sadi was unprejudiced and believing in heart, he proclaimed the doctrine that Buddhas alone have gained: The Four Noble Truths: The Fact of Suffering, its Cause, its Cessation, and the Noble Eightfold Path. As a clean cloth from which stains have been washed away will take the dye, so Pokkhara-sadi while sitting there obtained the spotless Eye for the Truth. He cried: This is most excellent, O Gotama, as if a man were to put up what had been thrown down and bring a lamp into the darkness. I go to Gotama as my guide, to the Teaching and the Order, may he accept me as a disciple as long as life endures.

XXXIII

A SCHOLAR named Sona-danda, who dwelt on a royal domain, heard that Gotama was staying by a lakeside and had a great reputation, and he decided to go there. But there were five hundred priests from other places and they came to protest that if he did so

Sona-danda's reputation would decrease and Gotama's would increase. They gave many other reasons, such as that Sona-danda was well born on both sides, was prosperous, and had mastered the sacred verses, knew the three Vedas, ritual, exegesis, legends and grammar. He was handsome, virtuous, long-lived, honoured and a teacher of teachers. For all these reasons he should not call on Gotama but Gotama should call on him.

* XXXIV *

WHEN THE PRIESTS had said this, Sona-danda replied: Now listen why it is fitting that I should call on the venerable Gotama and not he on me. He is well born on both sides, but gave up much treasure to go forth to the homeless life. He is handsome, virtuous, a teacher of teachers. He believes in Karma and right action. He has all the marks of a great man, a high reputation, and many heavenly beings trust him. He bids all men welcome and wherever he stays animals do men no harm. He is the head of an Order, many kings with their families and people believe in him, his reputation comes from perfect conduct and righteousness, and it is fitting that I should call on him.

* XXXV *

SONA-DANDA went to see the Buddha with a great company of priests, but on the way these hesitations arose in his mind: If I ask Gotama a question and he says it ought to be framed in a different way, people will think I am foolish and my reputation will decrease. And if he asks me a question he may not approve of my answer, but if I turn back people will think I am afraid. So he came slowly to the Buddha and greeted him, but the Buddha was aware of his hesitations and decided to question him on his own teaching.

* XXXVI *

THE BUDDHA asked Sona-danda: What are the things that priests say a man ought to have in order to be a true scholar? Sona-danda replied: They say he must have five things: good birth on both sides, knowledge of the Veda verses and ritual, beauty and fair colour, virtue, and wisdom. The Buddha asked: Is it possible to leave out one of these five things and declare the man who has the other four to be a true scholar? He answered: Yes, we could leave out colour, for what does that matter if he has good birth, ritual training, virtue and wisdom? The Buddha continued: But can we leave out one of these four? He answered: Yes, we can leave out ritual training. The Buddha asked: Can we leave out one of the other three? He replied: Yes, we can leave out birth, for what does that matter if he has virtue and wisdom?

* XXXVII *

THE OTHER priests protested: Gotama is depreciating not only our colour, but our ritual training and birth, and you are going over to his teaching. The Buddha said: If you think Sona-danda is unwise then let him be quiet and one of you discuss with me. Then he said to Sona-danda: Is it possible to leave one of these two

41

things out, and declare the man who has the other to be a true scholar and priest? He answered: No, for wisdom is purified by uprightness and uprightness is purified by wisdom. Where there is one, there is the other. The Buddha replied: That is right, and I say the same.

★ XXXVIII ★

THERE WAS a priest named Sharp-Tooth who was preparing a sacrifice of many animals, and when he heard of the arrival of the Buddha in the woods he decided to go and ask him about further rituals for sacrifice. When he made his request the Master answered with this parable: Long ago there was a king named Wide-Realm who wished to offer sacrifice to ensure continued prosperity. He asked his chaplain how it might be done and he said: There are many bandits about and if you impose new taxes or threats of death that will not stop them. But if you give away food and seed corn, and capital to traders, everyone will follow his own business and not harass others. And so it was. Everyone did his work, the land became peaceful, and the people and their children were happy.

★ XXXIX ★

KING WIDE-REALM saw that disorder was ended and asked his chaplain how he should sacrifice now. The chaplain said: There will come to your sacrifice men who destroy life and men who do not, men who steal and men who are honest, men who do evil and men

42

who do good. Let your majesty leave the evil alone with their evil, and offer only for those who do well.

Then at that sacrifice no animals were killed, no beasts or fowls. No trees were cut down or sacred grass mown. The workmen were not driven by sticks or fear or worked with tears. Each one did what he chose, and left what he did not choose. Ministers and householders were sent back with their gifts, and the sacrifice was accomplished in peace.

★ XL ★

THE PRIEST Sharp-Tooth asked: Does the venerable Gotama agree that one who makes such a sacrifice will be reborn into a happy state in heaven? The Buddha replied: Yes, for I myself was that chaplain in a previous life. Sharp-Tooth asked: Is there any sacrifice less difficult but more beneficial than this? The Master answered: Yes, gifts to virtuous ascetics are better. Sharp-Tooth asked: Is there a better sacrifice? The Buddha replied: Yes, providing a shelter for the Order is better. Sharp-Tooth asked: Is there any better sacrifice? The Buddha said: Yes, taking the Buddha as his guide, with the Teaching and Order. Sharp-Tooth asked: Is there any better sacrifice? The Buddha said: Yes, following the Five Precepts: not to kill, steal, lust, lie, or drink intoxicants.

★ XLI ★

THE BUDDHA was staying in a gabled hall in a wood when a man named Hare-Lip came to him and asked: Three years ago a disciple came to you and now claims

43

that he can see divine forms and hear sounds. Are they real or have they no existence? The Buddha replied: They are real, not things of nothing. Hare-Lip asked: What then is the cause of hearing or seeing heavenly things? The Buddha said: It comes from concentration on heavenly forms or sounds. Hare-Lip said: Then is it for the sake of such concentration that men take up the religious life with you? The Buddha answered: No, there are higher and sweeter things for which they do it. If a brother is converted by the destruction of the Three Bonds, of self and doubt and ceremonies, he cannot be reborn in sorrow and he attains to the insight of high stages.

★XLII★

THE BUDDHA told Hare-Lip further: If a brother destroys those Three Bonds, and reduces lust and ill-will to a minimum, then if he is reborn into this world he will make an end of pain. And if he destroys these Five Bonds he will never return to earth. If he destroys the Deadly Floods of lusts and ignorance he abides in freedom of heart and mind. Hare-Lip asked: Is there a method for realizing that state? The Buddha replied: Yes, there is the Noble Eightfold Path.

★XLIII★

THE BUDDHA was staying in a deer-park when Kassapa, a naked ascetic, greeted him and said: I have heard, O Gotama, that you disparage austerity and find fault with every ascetic. Is this true or false? The Buddha replied: Those who said so were reporting me falsely,

44

for I approve of some things and not of others. If a man goes naked and has loose habits, licking his hands clean, eating filth or only twice a month, sleeping on the ground or on thorns, and many such practices, if he does all this and is not disciplined in conduct, heart and mind, he is far from discipleship. But if he cultivates a heart of love, without anger or ill-will, free from intoxications of lusts, then already in this world he is a true disciple and scholar.

★ XLIV ★

THERE WAS a wandering beggar, Potthapada, staying in a hall which had been built in the Queen's Park for discussion of different opinions, and with him were three hundred others. One morning they were talking in loud voices about kings and robbers, food and clothes, beds and perfumes, women and heroes, ghosts and terrors. It was like street corner gossip, as well as speculations on existence and non-existence. Now the Buddha prepared to go out with his bowl for alms, but when Potthapada saw him he called the assembly to order saying: Here is the venerable Gotama who delights in peace and quiet. If we are quiet perhaps he will join us.

★ XLV ★

AS IT WAS EARLY the Buddha entered the hall and Potthapada put ten questions to him, the Ten Indeterminates: Is the world eternal? Is it not eternal? Is it finite? Or infinite? Is the soul the same as the body? Is it different? Does one live again after death? Or not live again? Or both live again and not live again? Or neither live again nor not live again? To each question the Buddha answered: That is a matter on which I have not expressed an opinion. Potthapada asked: Why? The Buddha replied: That question does not profit, it is not concerned with the Truth, or help right conduct, or detachment, or purification, or quiet, or tranquillity, or real knowledge. It does not lead to the higher stages of the Path or to Nirvana. That is why I express no opinion on it.

★ XLVI ★

THE BUDDHA rose and went away on his alms-tour, and those beggars broke into a torrent of jeering, shouting bitterly at Potthapada: You accept whatever Gotama says but we see that he has no distinct doctrine on any of the ten points raised. Potthapada replied: I agree that he puts forward no certain proposition on these points, but he does lay down a method in accordance with the nature of things, right and fitting and based on the truth. I could not refuse to approve what he said so well about that.

★ XLVII ★

TWO OR THREE days later Potthapada came to where the Buddha was staying and told him how the others had jeered. The Buddha said: They are blind and you are the only one with eyes to see. The Ten Indeterminates that you raise I hold to be uncertain, but the Four Noble Truths I hold to be certain. The Buddha continued: There are some scholars who speculate that the soul is perfectly happy after death. But when I asked them if people in this world are perfectly happy they answered, No. And when I asked if they had been perfectly happy even for half a day they said, No. And when I asked if they knew a method for realizing a perfectly happy state they said, No. So the talk of these scholars is groundless.

★XLVIII★

THE BUDDHA continued: It is like a man saying: How I long for and love the most beautiful woman in the land! And when people ask him: Does she belong to the class of nobles or priests, merchants or servants; is she tall or short, fair or dark; what is her name or family or town? He will answer that he does not know, and people will say: Then you have not seen the one that you long for. The talk of such a man is foolish, and so it is of those scholars who talk about the soul being perfectly happy and healthy after death.

★XLIX★

THE BUDDHA was staying in a mango grove at Nalanda when a young householder, Kevaddha, came to salute him and said: Our city of Nalanda is prosperous and influential and it would be good if the Buddha were to command some brother to perform a miracle so that many more people might believe in him. The Buddha replied: I do not give instruction in this way, by telling my brothers to perform miracles to astonish the laity.

THE BUDDHA told Kevaddha that there are three sorts of miracles: There is the Miracle of Mysteries, by which man becomes invisible, passes through walls or walks on water. But an unbeliever might do this by a magical charm, and because I see the danger of such miracles I detest them. Then there is the Miracle of Secrets, by reading the hearts and minds of others and telling them what they are thinking. But this also might be done by a magical charm, and I detest it. Finally there is the Miracle of Education by which one hears the preaching of a Buddha, awakens to it, is disciplined in act and word and speech. One thus obtains joy and peace, realizes the Four Noble Truths, and the final assurance of the freedom of discipleship. This is the Miracle of Education.

THE BUDDHA was on tour and came to a village where lived a priest named Lohiccha, who believed that if one had attained a good state of mind he should tell nobody else about it for fear of being entangled again in lust. Lohiccha sent his barber to invite the Buddha and his disciples to a meal and when they came he served them with his own hands till they were full. Then the Buddha asked Lohiccha if his opinions were as reported and when he admitted it the Buddha said: Supposing one were to say that Lohiccha had property and enjoyed all its revenue and produce himself, would not that be against general welfare and show enmity to society? And if a king enjoyed all his revenue and produce, would not that be against general welfare? Then if one attains a good state of mind but tells no one else about it that is against general welfare, out of sympathy with others, and unsound doctrine.

* LII *

THE BUDDHA said to Lohiccha: There are three kinds of teachers who deserve blame. The first is one who has not attained to the Truth but teaches it to others, who neither listen nor practise it. The second has not attained but teaches it to others who practise it. The third has attained the Truth and teaches it to others, who neither listen nor practise it. Lohiccha asked: But is there a teacher who is not blameworthy? The Buddha replied: Yes, when a Buddha appears and one listens to his preaching, awakens to it, is disciplined in act and word and speech, realizes the Four Noble Truths and the attainment of discipleship. Whoever the teacher is, if the disciple attains such distinction under him, the teacher is not blameworthy.

* LIII *

TWO PRIESTS were taking exercise after their bath and discussing the true and false paths. Vasettha said: This is the straight path to salvation and union with the Creator. Bharadvaja said that his path did the same and neither could convince the other. Vasettha said: I have heard that the venerable Gotama, who left the Shakya clan to adopt the religious life, is staying in the mango grove and he has a great reputation. It is said

49

that he is fully enlightened, wise, good and happy, a guide to mortals, a teacher of gods and men, a Buddha. Let us go and ask him about this matter and consider his words.

★ LIV ★

VASETTHA AND BHARADVAJA asked the Buddha: Various priests teach various paths, but do they all save and lead to union with the Creator? Are they like paths to a village which all converge on it? The Buddha asked: Have any of these priests or their pupils, versed though they are in the scriptures, seen the Creator face-to-face? If not, they mean that they can show the way to union with what they have not seen. This is like a string of blind men, when neither the ones in front, nor the middle nor the back can see where they are going.

★ LV ★

THE BUDDHA said to Vasettha: Priests who are versed in the scriptures call upon the gods, but they omit to practise those qualities which really make a man a priest. There are five things which lead to lust, which are called chains and bonds in the Discipline of the Perfect. Vasettha asked: What are these five? The Buddha replied: There are forms desirable to the eye which are accompanied by lust. There are sounds of the same kind, and odours, tastes and substances. These five things lead to passion and are called chains and bonds.

THE BUDDHA asked Vasettha: Has the Creator wives and wealth or not? He replied: He has not. The Buddha continued: Is his mind full of anger or free from it? Is it tarnished or pure? Has he self-mastery or not? Vasettha replied: His mind is free from anger, pure and self-mastered. The Buddha said: But the priests have wives and wealth, anger and malice, and lack purity and self-mastery. It is not possible that they should be united with the Creator.

THE YOUNG PRIEST VASETTHA said: I have heard that the venerable Gotama knows the way to union with the Creator. The Buddha said: Is the mango grove near or distant? Vasettha answered: It is here. The Buddha asked: Suppose a man born here had never left and people asked him the way to the mango grove, would he be in any doubt or difficulty? Vasettha replied: No, every road would be familiar to him. The Buddha said: That man might have some difficulty, but for the Buddha there can be no doubt about the path which leads to the world of the Creator, for I know it as one who has entered it and has been born in it.

VASETTHA said: Let the Buddha show us the way to union with the Creator and save us. The Buddha replied: From time to time there appears a fully enlightened one in the world, a guide to mortals, a teacher of gods and men, a Buddha. If a householder or a man of lower birth in any class has faith in him, renounces the world and adopts the homeless life, he is upright in word and deed. His conduct is good, he is free from malice and master of himself. He lets his mind pervade the world with thoughts of love. That is the way to union with the Creator.

★ LIX ★

THE BUDDHA said: Such a brother is free from anger and malice, pure and self-mastered, and the Creator is the same. That such a brother should be united with the Creator after death is fully possible. The two young priests Vasettha and Bharadvaja cried: This is most excellent, as if a man were to put up what had been thrown down, so the truth has been made known to us in many a figure. Now we go to the Blessed One as our guide, to the Truth and the Order. May he accept us as disciples and true believers, from this day forth as long as life endures.

★ LX ★

WHEN Vasettha and Bharadvaja were passing their probation among the brothers the Buddha said: You are Brahmin priests by birth and you have left home for a wandering life, do not your fellow priests blame you? Vasettha replied: Yes they revile us copiously. They say that priests are the best social grade, of pure breed and children of the gods, and that we have gone over to the lower classes of shaven friars, dark inferiors and vulgar servants. The Buddha remarked: There are four classes: nobles, priests, merchants and servants. But sometimes a noble kills a man, or is a thief, or unchaste, or a liar or malevolent. These are unworthy qualities, and the same may be said of priests, merchants and servants. Good and bad qualities are distributed among all classes and the wise do not admit claims of superiority.

The Doctrine is best throughout the world,
in this life and the next.

★ LXI ★

The Buddha went to stay on a Vulture Peak in Rajagaha. Then king Ajata-sattu of Magadha decided to attack his enemies the Vajjians, but before doing so he called his prime minister and said: Go to the Buddha and tell him I am about to attack the Vajjians, and take careful note of what he says for he only speaks the truth. When the minister arrived Ananda was standing behind his master fanning him, and the Buddha said: Have you heard, Ananda, that the Vajjians often hold public meetings of their clan? As long as they meet in concord and respect the rights of men and women they will prosper. Then he said to the minister: I taught the Vajjians the conditions of welfare and as long as they respect them they will not decline. The minister replied: Then the Vajjians cannot be overcome. And he went away pleased with the Buddha's words.

LXII

ANANDA came and bowed to the Buddha and sat at his side, saying: Your teaching on events arising from causes is wonderful, it looks and is so deep, and yet to me it seems as clear as can be. The Buddha retorted: Do not say that, Ananda, for this doctrine of events arising from causes both looks and is deep. It is because this generation does not understand this teaching that it has become a tangled skein, a matted ball of thread, a mass of grass and rushes, unable to avoid the doom, the waste, the way of sorrow, the constant round of transmigration.

LXIII

ANANDA ASKED: How are members of the Order to conduct themselves towards women? The Buddha replied: As if they did not see them. Ananda asked: But if we see them, what are we to do? The Buddha answered: Do not speak. Ananda persisted: But if they speak to us, what are we to do? The Buddha said: Keep wide awake.

LXIV

THE BUDDHA taught the brothers methods of meditation saying: The only way that leads to purification, passing beyond grief, extinguishing misery and realizing Nirvana is the Fourfold Setting Up of Mindfulness. What are these four? Let a brother so look on his body that he overcomes desires and despair, and remains self-possessed and mindful. And in the same way let him look upon feelings, thoughts and ideas. Let a brother going into the forest, or to the foot of a tree or into an empty room, sit down cross-legged, holding his body erect and make his mindfulness alert. Let him breathe in and out mindfully and be conscious of it. Let him practise with the thought of tranquillizing the body and its elements, externally and internally, its decay, coming to be and passing away. Similarly let him consider the passing nature of feelings, thoughts and ideas.

★ LXV ★

A DISCIPLE named Sunakkhatta came to the Buddha and said: Sir, I am leaving you and will no longer remain under you as my teacher. The Buddha inquired: Did I ever tell you to come and live under me as my pupil? He admitted: No, sir, you did not. The Buddha asked: Did you ever ask me that you might come and live under me? He replied: No, sir, I did not. The Buddha said: Then if I did not say the one and you did not say the other, what are you and what am I that you talk of giving up? Sunakkhatta said: Well, the Exalted One works no miracles beyond the powers of ordinary men. The Buddha answered: Whether wonders beyond the powers of ordinary men are performed or not, that is not the object for which I teach the Truth. The object of teaching the Truth is to destroy evil in the one who practises it.

★ LXVI ★

SUNAKKHATTA objected again: But, sir, you do not reveal to me the origins of the world. The Buddha asked: Did I ever tell you to be my disciple and I would reveal the origins of the world? He admitted: No, sir, you did not. The Buddha asked: Did you ever tell me that you would become my pupil so that I could reveal the origins of the world? He said: No, sir, I did not. The Buddha replied: Then if I did not say the one and you did not say the other, why do you talk of giving up discipleship on that account? Whether the beginnings of things is revealed or not, is not the object for which I teach the Truth, but it is to destroy evil in the one that practises it. But Sunakkhatta was not able to lead the holy life with the Buddha, he renounced the discipline and turned to lower things like one doomed to disaster and future suffering.

LXVII

NIGRODHA THE WANDERER was sitting in the Queen's Park with a large company of religious nomads, all talking in loud voices about kings and robbers, food and women, ghosts and speculations. He saw the householder Sandhana approaching and called the company to order, saying: Be still, here is a disciple of the venerable Gotama approaching and these gentlemen delight in quiet and are trained in it. When Sandhana arrived he was given a seat and Nigrodha asked him: Do you know with whom Gotama talks or gains lucidity in wisdom by conversation? His perception is ruined by his habit of seclusion, he is not at home in an assembly and he is not ready in conversation. Gotama is like a one-eyed cow walking in a circle, and if he were to come here we could settle him with a single question and roll him over like an empty pot.

THE BUDDHA with supernatural hearing knew of this conversation between Nigrodha the Wanderer and Sandhana the Householder as he was on the Vulture Peak. He came down to them and Nigrodha invited him to enter the house and take a seat. Nigrodha asked: What is this religion in which you train your disciples so that they acknowledge it to be their support and the principle of right? The Buddha answered: It is difficult for one of another view or confession to understand without practice and teaching the way in which I train my disciples. But ask me a question about your own doctrine or ascetic practices and the reasons for following or not following them. When he had said this the Wanderers cried loudly that it was wonderful for Gotama to withhold his own theories and discuss those of others.

NIGRODHA told the Wanderers to be quiet and said: We profess self-mortifying austerities and consider them to be essential. The Buddha asked: Suppose an ascetic is naked and has loose habits, licking his hands clean, eating filth or only twice a month, sleeping on the ground or on thorns, plucking out his hair and many such things, is his austerity self-mortification or not? Nigrodha replied: If these things are done that is the austerity of self-mortification. The Buddha answered: But I maintain that such austerity involves several defects. Such an ascetic becomes complacent, exalting himself and despising others, he becomes infatuated and careless, he attracts gifts and fame. People bring him presents and he becomes greedy and selective of foods. He expects kings and their officials to honour him and he envies others who receive their attention. In this and many other ways there are flaws in the austerities of self-mortification.

* LXX *

THE BUDDHA told Nigrodha: The austerity that wins to the topmost rank or reality, and reaches beyond the bark into the pith, is that of an ascetic who is self-restrained and has put away all hindrances. He has let his mind pervade the world with love, pity, sympathy and calm. With divine vision he sees himself and other beings passing from one existence to another. He recognizes the mean and the noble, the ugly and the beautiful, the wretched and the happy, passing away according to their deeds. He recognizes that those beings which are good in act, word and thought acquire Karma that results from right views and when their bodies are dissolved they are reborn into a happy state in heaven. This is the religion in which I train my disciples, so that they acknowledge it to be their support and the principle of righteous living.

* LXXI *

ON ANOTHER OCCASION the Buddha was staying in the mango grove of a family named the Archers. Now an ascetic teacher had just died and his followers were divided into two parties, quarrelling over doctrine and discipline. Even lay disciples were shocked at this dispute and one novice came to see Ananda and told him of the division. They decided that it was a worthy subject to bring before the Buddha so they told him about it. The Buddha said: Here we have a teacher who was not fully enlightened, a doctrine that was badly imparted, and a discipline that did not conduce to peace. In such teaching the disciple does not master the doctrine, or walk according to the precepts, for they are not conducive to peace.

★ LXXII ★

ONE OF the chief disciples was Sariputta, who praised the Buddha as he stayed in the mango wood near Nalanda, saying: I have such faith in the Exalted One that I think there never has been or will be or is now anyone who is greater and wiser than he. The Buddha remarked: These are great and bold words, like a lion's roar. Have you seen all the Exalted Ones of the past and future, with their conduct and doctrines? Sariputta said: No. The Buddha asked: Then why have you uttered this universal lion's roar? Sariputta answered: I have no knowledge of past, future or present Buddhas, but I only know what conforms to the Truth. It happened one day that while the Exalted One was expounding the Doctrine, each point more excellent than the last, I understood the Truth. And one doctrine was most perfect, namely faith in the Master. I confessed in my heart that the Exalted One is fully enlightened, his Doctrine is well taught, and his Order is blessed.

LXXIII

THE BUDDHA was staying near Rajagaha in a bamboo wood at a squirrels' feeding-ground. At that time a young householder, Sigala, rose up early and with wet hair and clothes he went out of Rajagaha. He lifted up his clasped hands and worshipped the quarters of the earth and sky: east and south, west and north, above and below. The Buddha on his alms-tour saw Sigala and asked why he worshipped in that manner. Sigala replied that his father when dying had told him to do so. The Buddha said: But in true religion worship should not be done in this way. Sigala asked: How then should worship be conducted in true religion? The Buddha answered: By putting away the four vices of conduct, which are killing, stealing, lust and lying. By avoiding evil actions one embraces the six quarters of earth and sky, conquers the world and is born to happiness in heaven.

LXXIV

THE BUDDHA instructed Sigala in the right conduct of a householder: There are six ways of dissipating wealth: addiction to intoxicants, wandering at unseemly hours, haunting fairs, gambling, having evil companions and idleness. There are four persons who are foes in the likeness of friends: the greedy, the speaker who does not act, the flatterer and the wastrel. There are four friends who are sound at heart: the helper, the counsellor, the sympathizer, and the one who is the same in happiness and adversity. There are six duties like the six quarters: to parents, teachers, friends, wife and children, servants and workers, and religious teachers.

* LXXV *

THE BUDDHA instructed Sigala in family duties: A child should minister to his parents in five ways: Once supported by them I will be their support, I will do my duty to them, maintain the lineage of my family, keep up its tradition, and be worthy of its heritage. Parents should love their child in five ways: restrain him from vice, exhort him to virtue, train him for a profession, arrange a suitable marriage for him, and give him the inheritance in due time. A husband should minister to his wife in five ways: by respect, courtesy, faithfulness, giving her authority, and adorning her. A wife loves her husband in five ways: by performing duties well, giving hospitality to both families, by faithfulness, by watching over his goods, and by skill and industry. A man should minister to his friends by generosity, courtesy and benevolence, treating them as he treats himself, and being as good as his word. They should love him by protecting him and his property, being a refuge in danger, faithful in trouble and considerate to his family.

* LXXVI *

THE BUDDHA instructed Sigala in social duties: Pupils should minister to their teachers in five ways: saluting

61

them, waiting on them, eagerness to learn, serving them, and attention to their teaching. Teachers should love their pupils in five ways: training them, making them hold it fast, teaching every art, speaking well of them, and providing for their safety. Masters should minister to their servants in five ways: giving work according to their strength, supplying food and wages, tending them in sickness, sharing delicacies with them, and giving them leave at times. Servants love their master in five ways: rising before him, going to rest after him, being content with what is given, working well, and showing his praise and fame. When the Buddha had finished Sigala cried: This is beautiful, setting up what was overthrown and shining a lamp in darkness. I go to the Exalted One as my refuge, to the Truth and the Order. May he receive me as a lay disciple who takes refuge in him as long as life endures.

LXXVII

THE BUDDHA taught the effect of mental attitudes upon action, saying: It is mind which gives things their quality, foundation and being. He who speaks or acts with an impure mind is followed by sorrow, as the wheel follows the steps of the ox. 'He insulted me, he struck me, he defeated me, he robbed me.' Those who harbour such thoughts never lose their hatred. 'He insulted me, he struck me, he defeated me, he robbed me.' Those who do not harbour such thoughts are freed from hatred. Hatred never ceases by hating, it ceases by not hating. That is the eternal law. Victory breeds enmity, for the conquered lie down in sorrow.

62

The calm man dwells in peace, beyond both victory and defeat.

* LXXVIII *

THE BUDDHA'S SON, Rahula, had left the palace for the homeless life, and one day as the Buddha set out on an alms-tour Rahula followed close behind. The Master, without looking round, said: All material forms, past, present and future, inside or out, gross or subtle, base or fine, far or near, should be viewed with full understanding. One should think: This is not mine, this is not I, this is not my self. Rahula asked: Only material forms? The Buddha answered: No, not only material forms, but also the other four elements of individuality—namely, feelings, perception, psychic dispositions and consciousness. Develop the state of mind of friendliness, Rahula, for as you do this ill-will grows less. Develop compassion and anger grows less, develop joy and aversion grows less, develop equanimity and dislike grows less.

* LXXIX *

THERE WAS a monk named Sati, the son of a fisherman, who thought wrongly that the Buddha taught of consciousness continuing throughout transmigration. When they heard this several brothers went and reasoned with him, but he would not give in. So they sent to the Buddha and put the matter to him and he sent for Sati. The Buddha asked: What is the nature of consciousness? Sati replied: It is that which speaks and feels, and experiences the consequences of good

63

and evil deeds. The Buddha exclaimed: You foolish fellow, whom do you tell that I have taught such a doctrine? Have I not said, with many examples, that consciousness is not independent but comes about through the Chain of Causation and cannot arise without a cause? Consciousness is caused by ignorance, but when there is a complete cessation of ignorance the whole body of suffering ceases.

LXXX

A STRICT vegetarian monk named Jivaka asked the Buddha: I have heard that men kill living creatures expressly for the venerable Gotama and that he eats such food. Is this true or in accordance with his Doctrine? The Buddha replied: It is not true, for meat may not be taken if it is seen, heard or suspected to have been killed on purpose for a monk. But it may be used if it is not seen, heard or suspected. A monk who depends on a village fills it with a mind of friendliness and if he is invited to a meal by a householder, he takes the food without being ensnared or entranced by it, but seeing its danger and the way of escape from lust. But he who kills a living creature for a Teacher or his disciple causes pain and distress to that creature and stores up much demerit. Jivaka replied: That is true and it is marvellous that the monks eat food that is allowable and blameless.

LXXXI

THE BUDDHA spoke a parable to the brothers, saying: A sower does not sow a crop for herds of deer thinking that they will enjoy it and flourish long in good condition, but he sows the crop thinking that the deer will eat it and be happy and get careless so that he can do to them as he will. Some deer eat the crop and become captive; others refuse it and plunge into the forest, but when grass and water give out they return to eat the sower's crop and are taken captive. Others are wily and eat near the crop but are finally taken by stakes and snares. But others make a lair where the sower cannot come and live in safety.

The meaning of the parable is that the sower is Mara, the deadly Tempter. His companions are Mara's companions, and the herds of deer are names for different classes of recluses, priests and monks. Some are entrapped by material things, and only those who refrain from their pleasures escape the mastery of Mara. One who abides in renunciation by wisdom and has destroyed all faults, has put a darkness round Mara and crossed over the entanglements of the world.

★ LXXXII ★

ON ANOTHER OCCASION the Buddha spoke to the brothers: Live as islands to yourselves, with the Doctrine and no other as your refuge. Keep to your own pastures where Mara will find no room for attack. For there will come a time when moral conduct will disappear and immorality will flourish. Men will lack filial and religious piety and show no reverence to female relations. The world will fall into promiscuity, like pigs and jackals; there will be enmity and animosity, and thought of killing even of parents by children and children by parents. Men will appear like wild beasts, and some will hide in holes in trees, in dens in the jungle and clefts in the mountains. But in time they will come out and embrace each other because they are still alive. Having done evil, they will now turn to good, abstain from taking life and increase in comeliness. They will learn to practise filial and religious piety and will prosper, with little disease but old age. Then will arise a Wheel-turning King who will rule in righteousness. And there will arise an Exalted One named Maitreya, full of wisdom and goodness, a guide for mortals, a teacher of gods and men, a Buddha, even as I am now. He will know the world with its men and princes, gods and demons, and will proclaim the Truth, lovely in its origin, progress and end, and make known the higher life as I do now.

LXXXIII

MOGGALLANA, one of the chief disciples, said to the brothers: If a monk invites me to speak to him there are some qualities that make it difficult to do so: if he is in bondage to evil desires, or exalts himself and disparages others, or is overpowered by wrath, or finds faults, or takes offence, or utters angry words, or shows temper, or is harsh, or spiteful, or treacherous, or seizes temporal things. But there are some qualities that make it easy to speak to a monk: if he does not exalt himself, is not proud, is not angry, is not in the grasp of evil desires, and so on. It is like a young man or woman looking at the reflection in a mirror. If one sees dust or blemish there he strives to get rid of it. But if he does not see dust or blemish and thinks he is clean he is in error. So a brother should forsake these evil unskilled states in the self by training night and day in skilled states.

KUMARA was declared by the Buddha to be the best preacher of the Order. He was ordained young and shone in faith in the Buddha like the full moon in mid-heaven. One day Kumara was walking on tour with about five hundred brothers and they met the chieftain Payasi who had an evil view of things. Payasi went to the grove where Kumara had stopped, greeted him, took a seat on one side, and declared: I am of the opinion that there is no other world, beings are not reborn, and there is no result of actions done well or ill. Kumara asked: What do you think? Are yonder sun and moon in this world or another? Payasi answered: They are in another world. Kumara said: Then let this be taken as evidence that there is another world.

PAYASI SAID: Even though Master Kumara says so, it still seems to me that beings are not reborn in another world. Kumara asked: Have you any proof to establish that they do not exist? Payasi replied: Here it is. I have had friends who have taken life, stolen, and committed other evil deeds, and they have fallen ill of mortal suffering. When I understood that they would not recover I asked them that if they were reborn into the Fallen Place, the Pit, as a result of their evil deeds, that they should come and tell me, or send a messenger to say so. But they have not done so, and this is evidence for me that there is no other world, or rebirth, or rewards of good and evil actions. Kumara replied: Suppose a felon was taken red-handed, bound tightly, paraded round the town, and taken to the place of execution. Now would this felon get permission from his executioners to wait until he had visited his friends and relatives and come back again? No, and this felon is human. How much less would your friends get permission from the keepers of the Pit to bring you back messages? And how much less would a good man wish to return from heaven to this place of suffering?

LXXXVI

PAYASI REPEATED: Even though Master Kumara says so, it still seems to me that none of these things exists. Kumara asked: Have you any further evidence? Payasi retorted: I have, for I see wanderers and scholars of moral and virtuous disposition and I think, if these good men knew that when we are dead we shall be better off, they would take poison or stab themselves or put an end to themselves in another way. But because they do not know that, they are fond of life and averse to sorrow and dying. Kumara replied: Suppose a pregnant woman took a sword and ripped up her belly to discover whether the child would be a boy or a girl. She would destroy both her own life and the unborn infant through this foolish action. Similarly you will meet with ruin by seeking for another world without wisdom. Virtuous men do not force maturity on what is unripe, but they wait for it because they are wise. The virtuous need their life, to produce merit for the welfare of many and out of compassion for the world, and this is a proof that there is a result of good and evil actions.

LXXXVII

PAYASI REPEATED: Even though Master Kumara says so, it still seems to me that none of these things exists. Suppose a felon was taken red-handed, thrown alive into a jar, its mouth covered with wet leather and clay, and put into a fire. When we knew the man was dead, we should open the jar quickly with the idea that we might see his soul coming out. But we do not see the soul coming out, and this is evidence for me that there is no other world or rebirth. Kumara replied: When you are taking a siesta you see dreams of gardens, groves and lakes. You are watched over by attendant women, but do they see your soul entering or leaving you? Let this be proof to you that these things do exist.

LXXXVIII

PAYASI REPEATED: Even though Master Kumara says so, it still seems to me that none of these things exists. I have had friends and kinsmen who kept the Five Precepts: abstained from taking life, unchastity, stealing, lying and strong drink. When they have fallen ill, I have told them that if they were reborn among the gods, or into another life, or with results of good deeds, they should come and tell me or send a messenger. But although they promised to do so they have not done it, and this is evidence for me that none of these things exists. Kumara said: You speak as a man born blind, who could not see objects or sun or moon, and were to say that none of these things exists. Payasi retorted: But these visual objects do exist and so does the faculty of seeing them. Kumara answered: The other world is not to be seen with the fleshly eye. Those wanderers and scholars who haunt the lonely recesses of the forest, purify their spiritual eye in discipline and solitude. By a purified spiritual vision, beyond the vision of men, they see both this world and the next. The spiritual world is seen in this way, and not by the fleshly eye as you imagine.

LXXXIX

KUMARA SAID: Renounce your evil set of opinions, and let them not be a source of sorrow to you. Payasi answered: I have been charmed by Master Kumara's similes from the first, for I wanted to hear his ready wit in questions. This is wonderful and marvellous, as if one were to set up what had been cast down, reveal what was hidden, point the road to the lost and bring a lamp into darkness, so that those who have eyes may see. And now I go for refuge to Gotama the Exalted One, to the Doctrine and the Order. May I be accepted as a disciple, as one who from this day forth has accepted this guidance as long as life endures, that it may bring me welfare and happiness.

70

✴ XC ✴

AS THE END of his life on earth drew near the Buddha told Ananda to assemble all the brothers from Rajagaha into a service hall, and he addressed them as follows: I will teach you Seven Conditions for the welfare of a community. The brothers must meet together often, they must agree and act in concord, they must not introduce something that has not been prescribed, or change something that has been established; they must honour and support the elders of the Order and listen to their words, they must not fall under the influence of that craving which leads to rebirth, and they must train their minds to be self-possessed so that others will come to them and be at ease. So long as these Seven Conditions exist among the brothers they may expect to prosper and not decline.

✴ XCI ✴

THE BUDDHA went on to a village where the lay disciples invited him to their rest-house. They strewed it with fresh sand, placed seats, set up a water-pot and fixed an oil lamp. When the Buddha arrived he washed his feet, entered the hall, and sat down against the centre pillar facing east. The brothers sat against the western wall, also facing east, and the lay disciples sat opposite the Buddha facing west. The Buddha said: O householders, there is a Fivefold Loss to a wrong-doer through lack of rectitude; he becomes poor through idleness, gets a bad reputation, enters shy and confused into society of any class, is full of anxiety when he dies, and is reborn to a state of suffering. But there

71

is a Fivefold Gain to a well-doer through practice
of rectitude; he becomes rich through hard work, gains
a good reputation, enters confidently into society of
any class, dies without anxiety, and is reborn into a
happy state in heaven.

* XCII *

THE BUDDHA went on to Vesali and stayed in the
mango grove of a courtesan named Ambapali. When
she heard that he had arrived Ambapali ordered her
state carriage and went as far as the ground was
passable, then continued on foot to where the Buddha
was, and took her seat respectfully on one side. She
listened to his words with gladness and said: Will the
Exalted One do me the honour of taking his meal at
my house tomorrow together with the brothers? And
the Buddha gave his consent by silence. Ambapali
arose and went home, and towards morning she
prepared a meal of sweet rice and cakes. When the
Buddha came she waited on him and his disciples till
they would take no more. Then Ambapali the
courtesan had a low stool brought and sat down beside
the Buddha and said: Lord, I present this place to the
Order of brothers of which the Buddha is chief. The
Buddha accepted the gift, and after instructing and
pleasing her with religious talk he rose from his seat
and went away.

* XCIII *

WHEN the rainy season came the Buddha fell seriously
ill, with sharp pains even unto death, but he was

mindful and self-possessed and bore the pains without complaint. By a strong effort of will he kept his hold on life till the time he fixed on should come, and when he recovered he came out from his lodging and sat in the shade. Then Ananda came and saluted him, saying: I have seen the Exalted One in health and sickness, and though the sight of his illness made me as weak as a creeper, I took comfort from the thought that he would not pass away until he had left instructions for the Order. The Buddha replied: What does the Order expect? I have preached the Truth without any distinction of open or secret doctrine, for I have no such thing as the closed fist of a teacher who keeps things back. I am old and my journey is drawing to a close, I am eighty years of age and my body is like a worn out cart. Why should I leave instructions for the Order? Be lamps to yourselves, seek no external refuge. Hold fast to the Truth as a lamp, hold fast to the Truth as a refuge.

* XCIV *

THE BUDDHA rose early, put on his robe and took his bowl, and went into Vesali for alms. When he had made his round and finished eating the rice he said to Ananda: Take up the mat, for I will spend the day at the shrine. Ananda did so and followed the Exalted One step by step, spreading out his mat and sitting respectfully at his side. The Buddha said: What a delightful place is Vesali with its shrines! Anyone who has practised the ways to perfection and mastered them could remain in the same birth for a whole age. I have

73

thoroughly practised and developed these ways, so that I could stay here for an age, or whatever part of an age is still to run, should I wish it. But although the Buddha gave this clear hint three times, Ananda did not plead with him to remain for the rest of the age and after a time he went to sit under a tree nearby.

* XCV *

NOT LONG after Ananda had gone Mara, the deadly Tempter, came and stood beside the Buddha saying: Pass away now, Lord, now is the time to die, for you said you would not die until the brothers and sisters of the Order, and male and female lay disciples, had become well trained in the teaching, establishing it and telling it to others. Now, Sir, the brothers and sisters have become all this and can do it, so let the Exalted One pass away, for the time has come and this pure religion is widespread. When Mara had spoken the Buddha answered: You may be happy, Mara, for the death of the Buddha will take place soon and at the end of three months he will pass away.

* XCVI *

SO THE BUDDHA deliberately and consciously rejected the rest of his natural term of life. He called Ananda and the brothers and said: Behold, all composite things must grow old. Work out your salvation with diligence, for in three months your Master will die.

My age is ripe, my life will close,
I leave and trust myself alone;

Be full of thought, in firmness stay,
be earnest, watch your hearts, your own;
for he who holds this Truth and Way
shall cross life's sea and end his woes.

★ XCVII ★

THE BUDDHA proceeded with many brothers till they came to a mango grove belonging to Chunda, a metal-worker. Chunda saluted the Master, sat down on one side and listened to his teaching. Gladdened by his words he besought the Buddha to take a meal at his house, and the Master gave consent by silence. At the end of the night Chunda made ready sweet rice and cakes and a quantity of pork and when the Buddha came in the morning he served him with the food. When he had tasted it, the Buddha said: Whatever pork is left over bury in a hole, for I see no one in heaven and earth who could digest that food. Chunda buried the pork, but upon the Master there came a grave sickness, dysentery and sharp pains even unto death. But being mindful and self-possessed he bore it without complaint.

★ XCVIII ★

THE BUDDHA said to Ananda: Let us go on to Kusinara. But on the way he turned aside and rested under a tree asking Ananda: Please fold the robe in four and spread it out for me, for I am tired and must rest awhile. Ananda did so and the Buddha asked: Please fetch me some water, for I am thirsty and must drink. But Ananda objected: Just now about five hundred carts passed through that stream and it has become dirty, wait till we get a little further on where there is a river with clear and cool water. But the Buddha told Ananda a second and third time to fetch water from the stream, and when he finally obeyed the stream which had been muddy was flowing clear and bright. Then Ananda took water in a bowl and took it to the Master, saying: How wonderful is the Buddha's power, for this stream which just now was muddy has become clear and bright. Let the Master drink the water. Let the Happy One drink the water.

⋆ XCIX ⋆

THE BUDDHA and his company arrived near the jungle town of Kusinara and went to a grove beyond a river. There he said to Ananda: Please spread my couch between twin trees, with its head to the north, for I am weary and would lie down. When Ananda had done this the Master lay on his right side, with one leg on the other, mindful and self-possessed. All the trees were full of flowers out of season which fell on the Buddha and covered him reverently, while heavenly music sounded out of reverence for the successor of the Buddhas of old. Then the Buddha said: It is not thus that the Buddha is best honoured and revered, but the brother or sister who fulfils all duties, is correct in life and walks according to the teaching, is the one who honours and reveres the Buddha most worthily.

⋆ C ⋆

ANANDA SAID: In days gone by we stayed in various

places in the rainy season and we used to receive brothers and bring them to the Master, but when he has gone we shall not be able to do this. The Buddha replied: There are four places which the believer should visit with reverence. He asked: What are they? The Buddha said: The place where the Buddha was born, the place where he attained Enlightenment, the place where the kingdom of Right was set on foot, and the place where he finally passed away. Ananda asked: What are we to do with the Master's remains? The Buddha replied: Do not hinder yourselves by honouring the Master's remains, but be zealous on your own behalf. Devote yourselves to your own good, and be earnest and intent. There are wise and noble men who will honour the Buddha's remains.

★ CI ★

ANANDA went into a house and leaned against the lintel weeping at the thought: I am still a learner who has to work out his own perfection, and the Master who is so kind is about to pass away. The Buddha noticed his absence and sent another brother to call him who reported that he was weeping. When Ananda came the Master said: Enough, Ananda, do not be troubled or weep. I have told you many times that it is in the nature of everything near and dear to us that we must separate ourselves from them. Everything that is born contains within itself the necessity of dissolution. For a long time you have been very near to me by acts and words and thoughts of love, kind and good, that never varied and were beyond measure. You have done well, be earnest in effort and you too will soon be free from all delusion.

★ CII ★

ANANDA SAID: Let not the Master die in this little wattle-and-daub town Kusinara in the midst of the jungle. There are other great cities, like Benares or Rajagaha, where the Buddha might die and wealthy nobles, priests and believers would pay honour to his remains. The Buddha replied: Do not say that this is a wattle-and-daub town in the midst of the jungle, but go into Kusinara and tell the elders that this night, in the last watch, the final passing away of the Buddha will take place, lest they reproach themselves that they did not visit him in his last hours. Ananda went and told this to the elders of Kusinara, and some of them wept and tore their hair and fell on the ground crying:

The Exalted One is dying too soon,
the Happy One is passing away too soon,
the Light in the world is vanishing too soon!

Then they went and each family was presented in a group to the Buddha in the first watch of the night.

★ CIII ★

THERE WAS a wanderer named Subhadda who heard that the venerable Gotama was dying and he thought: Seldom do Buddhas appear in this world, the Able Enlightened Ones. I must go to Gotama and resolve my doubts. When he arrived Ananda said: Friend

78

Subhadda, do not trouble the Master, for he is weary. But the Buddha overheard this and called out for Subhadda to come with his questions. Subhadda asked: Have the leaders of religious companies all understood things according to their claims, or have they not? The Buddha replied: Leave their claims aside but listen to the truth. In whatever teaching or discipline the Noble Eightfold Path is not found, a man of true holiness is not found there either.

At twenty-nine I sought the Good
and worldly happiness forswore,
and then a pilgrim's path pursued
for fifty years and one year more,
thro' realms of Truth and Discipline
where I alone could Victory win.

★ CIV ★

THE BUDDHA spoke of old age: Look at this painted image, a wounded and diseased body, full of thoughts without stability. It is a citadel of bones plastered over with flesh and blood, while inside are old age and death, pride and deceit. As the splendid chariots of kings wear out so the body comes to old age, but the virtue of the good never ages and they teach it to one another. I have passed through many births searching for the builder of this dwelling without finding him and the round of births is painful. Now you are seen, O Builder, and you will never build the house again. All your rafters are broken and your ridge-beam is destroyed. My mind has attained the extinction of desires and is set on Nirvana.

★ CV ★

THE DYING BUDDHA said to Ananda: It may be that some of you will think that the word of the Master is ended and you have a Teacher no longer. But you should not look on it in this way. The Truth, and the rules of the Order, which I have set out and laid down for you, shall be your Teacher after I have gone. Then the Buddha addressed the brothers: It may be that there is some doubt or misgiving in the mind of some brother, as to the Buddha or the Teaching, the path or the method. Inquire freely, so that you do not reproach yourselves afterwards with the thought that you did not ask the Master when you were face to face with him. He said this three times but the brothers were silent for no one had any doubts.

★ CVI ★

THE BUDDHA said to the brothers: I exhort you now in these words: All composite things are decaying. Work out your salvation with diligence.

These were the last words of the Buddha. Then he entered into stages of rapture, passing to states in which the consciousness of sensations and of ideas had wholly passed away, and going beyond the stages of rapture he died at once.

★ CVII ★

When the Buddha died Ananda uttered this verse:

Then there was great dismay,
our hair stood up in its place
when the Buddha passed away
endowed with every grace.

Some of the brothers who were not yet free from their
passions wept and rolled on the ground, crying: The
Buddha has died too soon, the Happy One has passed
away too soon, the Light has gone out in the world too
soon! But those brothers who were free from passion
were composed and bore their grief calmly with the
thought: All composite things are impermanent, how
is it possible that they should not be dissolved? The
Buddha told us that it is in the very nature of all
things near and dear to us that we must separate
ourselves from them. Everything that is born contains
within itself the necessity of dissolution, so how could
it be possible that such a being should not be dissolved?

★ CVIII ★

THE ELDERS of Kusinara came to pay homage to the
remains of the Buddha, and after a day with dancing
and hymns, garlands and perfumes, they built a
funeral pyre and prepared a cairn for the relics. But
seven other towns sent messengers claiming the relics
and a dispute arose. Then an elder scholar declared:
Our Buddha used to teach forbearance, and it is
unseemly that division should arise over the remains of
him who was the best of beings. Let us unite in
harmony and make eight portions, in order that there
may be cairns for the relics in many places and men

may trust in the Light in the world. This was done and eight portions of relics were made of him who was the best of the best of men. Gods and kings and men bowed with clasped hands, for it is hard indeed to meet with a Buddha and only once in centuries does it happen.

REFERENCES

The sources of the sections are given in order.

I   Digha Nikaya, in *Dialogues of the Buddha*, trs. T. W. and C. A. F. Rhys Davids, II, pp. 4f., 40

II   Majjhima Nikaya, in *The Middle Length Sayings*, trs. I. B. Horner, III, pp. 164f.

III   Dialogues II, pp. 18ff.

IV   Middle Length I, pp. 204f.

V   ibid. 295, 207

VI   ibid. 207–9

VII   ibid. 209–10

VIII   ibid. 210–11, 297

IX   ibid. 300; Mahavastu, trs. J. J. Jones, II, pp. 119ff.

X   Mahavastu II, 126f.; Middle Length I, 211

XI   Middle Length I, 212f.

XII   ibid. 213f.

XIII   ibid. 215f.

XIV   Dialogues II, 337f.; Samyutta Nikaya, in *Kindred Sayings*, trs. C. A. F. Rhys Davids and F. L. Woodward, V, pp. 357f.

XV   ibid.

XVI   Kindred Sayings, III, pp. 59f.

XVII   Dialogues I, 1ff.

XVIII   ibid. 3ff.

XIX   ibid. 30ff.

XX   ibid. 43ff.

XXI   ibid. 65f.

XXII   ibid. 67f.

XXIII   ibid. 68ff.

XXIV   ibid. 77ff.

XXV   ibid. 93ff.
XXVI   ibid. 108ff.
XXVII   ibid. 112ff.
XXVIII ibid. 123
XXIX   ibid. 125ff.
XXX   ibid. 132f.
XXXI   ibid. 133f.
XXXII   ibid. 135
XXXIII ibid. 144ff.
XXXIV   ibid. 147ff.
XXXV   ibid. 151f.
XXXVI   ibid. 152ff.
XXXVII ibid. 154ff.
XXXVIII ibid. 173ff.
XXXIX   ibid. 176ff.
XL   ibid. 181f.
XLI   ibid. 197ff.
XLII   ibid. 201f.
XLIII   ibid. 223ff.
XLIV   ibid. 244f.
XLV   ibid. 254f.
XLVI   ibid. 255f.
XLVII   ibid. 256f.
XLVIII ibid. 258f.
XLIX   ibid. 276
L   ibid. 277ff.
LI   ibid. 288ff.
LII   ibid. 293ff.
LIII   ibid. 301f.
LIV   ibid. 303f.
LV   ibid. 310f.

LVI   ibid. 313f.

LVII   ibid. 315

LVIII   ibid. 315f.

LIX   ibid. 318f.

LX   Dialogues III, pp. 77ff.

LXI   Dialogues II, pp. 78ff.

LXII   ibid. 50f.

LXIII   ibid. 154

LXIV   ibid. 327f.

LXV   Dialogues III, 8f.

LXVI   ibid. 9f.

LXVII   ibid. 33f.

LXVIII   ibid. 35f.

LXIX   ibid. 37ff.

LXX   ibid. 46f.

LXXI   ibid. 111f.

LXXII   ibid. 95ff.

LXXIII   ibid. 173

LXXIV   ibid. 175ff.

LXXV   ibid. 180f.

LXXVI   ibid. 181f.

LXXVII   Dhammapada, trs. S. Radhakrishnan, pp. 58ff.

LXXVIII   Middle Length II, 91ff.

LXXIX   Middle Length I, 311ff.

LXXX   Middle Length II, 32ff.

LXXXI   Middle Length I, 194ff.

LXXXII   Dialogues III, 59ff.

LXXXIII   Middle Length I, 124f.

LXXXIV   Dialogues II, 349f.

LXXXV   ibid. 351ff.

LXXXVI   ibid. 357f.

LXXXVII   ibid. 358f.

LXXXVIII   ibid. 355f.

LXXXIX   ibid. 370

XC   ibid. 81f.

XCI   ibid. 90f.

XCII   ibid. 102ff.

XCIII   ibid. 106f.

XCIV   ibid. 110ff.

XCV   ibid. 112f.

XCVI   ibid. 128

XCVII   ibid. 137f.

XCVIII   ibid. 139ff.

XCIX   ibid. 149f.

C   ibid. 153f.

CI   ibid. 157f.

CII   ibid. 161ff.

CIII   ibid. 164ff.

CIV   Dhammapada pp. 108f.

CV   Dialogues II, 171f.

CVI   ibid. 173f.

CVII   ibid. 177

CVIII   ibid. 180ff.